CIPS Study

Level

Advanced Diploma in Purchasing and Supply

PASSNOTES

Machinery of Government

© Profex Publishing Limited, 2010

Printed and distributed by the Chartered Institute of Purchasing & Supply
Easton House, Easton on the Hill, Stamford, Lincolnshire PE9 3NZ
Tel: +44 (0) 1780 756 777
Fax: +44 (0) 1780 751 610
Email: info@cips.org
Website: www.cips.org

First edition October 2010

Contents

Preface

Welcome to your **Passnotes**!

This element of your Study Pack has been specially designed to support you in your exam revision.

- Small-format **Passnotes** fit easily into a bag or briefcase: **convenient to use** wherever and whenever you have a few minutes for topic review or exam revision.

- The material is organised in **short, clearly labelled units**: easy to work through systematically or to dip into at any point, if that's what you prefer.

- Each area of the unit content starts with a simple **mind-map** of the relevant Learning Objectives, helpfully **cross-referenced** to chapters in your Course Book (so you can quickly locate more substantial topic coverage, if you need to refresh your memory).

- The units cover each (and all) of the **Learning Objectives** in turn (again, cross-referenced to other units where topics overlap), so you can see exactly what knowledge and understanding underpins potential exam questions.

- Within each unit, the material is presented in a format specially designed for **ease and speed of learning** — essential in the revision stage of your studies! **Passnotes** use key definitions, point lists, action plans, tables and diagrams:

  - To keep the topic coverage as focused and brief as possible
  - To offer an easily grasped overview of each topic
  - To make the topic more visual — and therefore (for most people) more readily memorable.

- For relevant topics, we also include Integrated Learning Checklists: point lists and action plans gathered from different Learning Objectives to give you a broader handle on topics, processes and management challenges. (Particularly useful for case study questions...)

Of course, Passnotes don't give you substantial or comprehensive coverage of the unit content. (That's what your **Course Book** is for.) What they do give you is **systematic and focused coverage**: a concise, easy-to-remember survey of the key points on which you can base an exam answer. This makes them ideal to use in the weeks and days leading up to the exam!

And don't forget: updates, case studies, advice on exam technique and other revision-support resources (including practice questions with full solutions) will be regularly added to the study resources.

Good luck.

1.1
Principles
and process
for public procurement

Course Book Chapter 1

- *Transparency*
- *Competition*
- *Political expediency*
- *Favouritism*
- *Fraud*

1.2
Impact of policies on role
and significance of
procurement

Course Book Chapter 2

- *Contracting out of services*
- *Private Finance Initiative*
- *Best Value*

1.3
Implementing private sector
best practice procurement
in the public sector

Course Book Chapter 3

- *Partnerships*
- *Supply chain management*
- *Cost reduction*
- *Innovation*
- *Professional competencies*

1.0
Background to
public
procurement
policy and
procedures

1.4
Traditional public
accountability systems to
act as a constraint on
improvement

Course Book Chapter 3

- *Government accounting cycle*
- *Annual budgeting*
- *Accounting Officer*
- *Internal/external audit*
- *Public Accounts Committee*

Transparency and competition in letting contracts

Competition Transparency (openness to audit) Procurement professionalism	**v**	Political expediency Economic survival of UK companies Favouritism Fraud/corruption

- ☑ Avoid accusations of favouritism
- ☑ Compliance with competition principles/laws (eg Article 85, 86 of Treaty of Rome)
- ☑ Strengthen protections against fraud/corruption
- ☑ Procurement efficiencies: value for money arising from competition
- ☑ Wider supplier participation: increased competition > increased competitiveness
- ☑ Avoidance of supplier complacency in 'cosy relationships' > declining competitiveness

EU Public Procurement Directive

Apply to purchasing by public bodies *unless* below a **financial threshold**.

Advertising	Subject to certain exceptions, public bodies must advertise invitation to tender according to rules designed to secure maximum publicity.

Contract award procedures and time limits	• **Open procedure:** no requirement for pre-qualification of suppliers. • **Restricted procedure:** pre-qualification of suppliers permitted, but contracting authority must indicate predetermined range of suppliers. • **Negotiated procedure:** must be justified (eg by urgency, additional contract, technical reasons, exclusive rights, no appropriate tenders). • **Competitive dialogue** to identify potential solutions and gradually reduce number of tenders to be negotiated: must be justified.

Award criteria	• Buyers generally obliged to award contract on basis of **lowest price** *or* **most economically advantageous tender** (best value) • All tenderers must have reasonable, equal and *timely* **information** re criteria and weighting (or ranking) of **non-price criteria**

Limitations/inflexibilities of competitive tendering

- ☒ In practice, little increase in non-national contract awards (Cox, Furlong)
- ☒ Little pre-qualification of bidders > potential risk
- ☒ MEAT criteria may undervalue non-price criteria eg sustainability
- ☒ Increased transaction cost (eg to justify competitive dialogue)
- ☒ Prevents development of partnership relations, strategic collaboration

>> Improving transparency

- **E-procurement** tools to increase transparency of competitive processes: identical information simultaneously disseminated

>> Achieving sustainable competition

Contingency approaches >> buyer/supplier relationship appropriate to purchase.

- **Purchase portfolio** (Kraljic): competitive for leverage/non-critical items; partnership for strategic/bottleneck items

- **Relational competence** (Cox): competitive for residual competencies; partnership for core/complementary competencies.

- **Best Value policy**: non-competitive letting of service contracts, where outcomes represent best value.

- **Partnership within competition.** Long-term partnering arrangements, *established* by competition and *re-opened* periodically to competition. NB: need to negotiate on-going competitiveness, innovation, cost and quality improvement over life of contract.

Use of public procurement for political purposes

Inevitable political dimension, due to significance of public expenditure, performance of national/local industry and desire of politicians for re-election.

| 'Procurement decisions should be made solely on commercial considerations.' | v | 'Procurement decisions may be used to further socio-economic goals.' |

- Preference for local/national suppliers, regions, SMEs or minority-owned suppliers
- Supporting environmental protection and sustainability
- Protecting employment, wage levels and conditions of employment
- Pursuing industry development (eg shipbuilding, defence, national champions)

☑ Wider socio-economic, industrial and sustainability benefits are in national interest
☑ Capacity building (eg by supporting SMEs, diverse suppliers, sustainability measures)
☑ Governments are mandated to use public procurement to pursue objectives
☑ Increasing value/scope of public procurement: must be used to support wider goals
☑ Other countries do not 'play by the rules': national self-interest required

☒ Distorts competition > uncompetitive supply and lack of VFM
☒ Discrimination (eg v non-national suppliers) is illegal under EU regulations
☒ Using contracts to 'buy votes' is an abuse of the democratic system
☒ National self interest threatens global free trade.

>> Policy objective: remove obstacles to *participation* in *competitive* processes.

Regularity, propriety and VFM

❑ **Regularity**: compliance with appropriate authorities

❑ **Propriety**: standards of conduct and corporate governance; fairness and integrity; avoiding personal profit from public business; avoiding waste and extravagance

❑ All public procurement of goods and services must be **based on VFM**, having due regard to **propriety and regularity** (OGC).

Protecting against fraud

Treasury Fraud Report (2004/5):

- ❏ Identify areas most vulnerable to fraud
- ❏ Put in place measures to manage fraud risk proportional to risks faced
- ❏ Allocate responsibility for managing fraud risk
- ❏ Have a fraud policy and response plan
- ❏ Establish avenues for staff to report suspicion of fraud
- ❏ Measure the effectiveness of anti-fraud processes
- ❏ Promote anti-fraud culture

How fraud committed	Example controls
Unauthorised use of purchasing systems to misappropriate goods	• Sequentially numbered purchase order forms • Authorised signatories + authorisation limits • Invoice/order matching, stock records • Separation of duties • Budgetary control and management checks
Acceptance of short deliveries	• Random management checks on deliveries
Acceptance of unsolicited goods or expanded orders (eg free gifts)	• Payment only made after confirmation that goods properly ordered/authorised
Misuse of procurement cards	• Designated cardholders, cardholder manager • Approvals by (separate) budget holder • Use of reputable/contracted suppliers • Policy/advice on use of cards • Statement checking, discrepancy reporting
Contractor selected by favouritism	• Clear, comprehensive, agreed specifications • Administer compliant tendering process

Obtaining value for money (VFM)

VFM is 'the optimum combination of whole life cost and quality to meet the customer's requirements' (1995 White Paper).

NB: balance **economy** (eg price reduction/avoidance) with **efficiency + effectiveness** (eg greater quantity/quality for same cost; improved delivery/performance).

Failure to provide VFM, due to:	Achieving VFM in procurement
Inadequate project management	Reduced processing overheads
Inadequate financial/risk appraisal	Better VFM for goods/services purchased
Inadequate validity re-appraisal	Better project/contract/asset management
Failure to use competition principles	Long-term VFM (not lowest price) thinking
Conflicts of interest when using private sector consultants	Leveraging e-commerce and good procurement practice
Failure to manage PFI refinancing	Using tools to promote/measure VFM gains

Historical role and significance of procurement

Central government:

- ❑ Pressures on public expenditure since 1976 >> new emphasis on achieving greater economy, efficiency, effectiveness (Financial Management Initiative)

- ❑ Adoption of 'external resource management' view (Lamming) from manufacturing sector >> recognition of potential strategic contribution

- ❑ 1979ff: shift from direct service provision towards market based competition and contractual relationships >> increasing procurement involvement in awarding service contracts (internal/external) + competitive tendering policy

- ❑ *Government Purchasing* (1984): impetus for development of specialist procurement function in central govt >> departmental procurement strategies; training of procurement staff; annual procurement savings targets; body of guidance on practice

- ❑ *Setting New Standards* (1995) >> increased focus on supplier/contract management

Local government:

- ❑ Expansion of role from clerical focus (order placing, expediting) > core function (achieving policy objectives + VFM)

- ❑ Debate re market's ability to provide services; competing values of efficiency/equity

Market provision of public services   (Entwhistle *et al*)

Without market discipline (competition), the State cannot deliver services efficiently: no incentive to control costs. 1979ff: shift to alternative governance structures.

Outcome of market test or compulsory competitive tender (CCT) may be:

Retain service in-house	Contract out to private sector contractor	Contract out to voluntary sector provider	'Mixed economy' provision

Transaction cost economics *(Williamson & Ouchi)*	**Principal-agent theory** *(Donahue)*
Make/buy decision should be determined by comparison of transaction costs. Internal provision suited to: recurrent exchanges, uncertain conditions, transaction-specific investments.	Successful contracting requires principal/client control over agent. Contracting suitable where: exact specifications, easily measured outputs, quick replacement of inadequate suppliers

Contestable markets	**Functional matching**
Inefficiency due to monopoly supply: need to create competitive pressures, service user choice. • Mixed provision (internal, private, voluntary)	Make/buy decision made on basis of different functional attributes/strengths of different sectors. • Allocate functions to most suitable sectors (internal, private, voluntary)

5

Internal provision advisable:	External/market provision advisable:
Recurrent exchange, in conditions of uncertainty, incurring transaction-specific investments *(Williamson & Ouchi)*	Because of the inefficiency of monopoly supply, with no internal incentives to control costs
Where responsiveness, local knowledge and political judgement are required	Where it is cheaper to buy one-off services (eg construction) than maintain capacity
Where future needs/priorities cannot be predicted with certainty	Supported by exact specifications, measurable outputs and ease of supplier replacement *(Donahue)*
Outputs are difficult to specify/measure	
With clear understanding of strengths of different sectors	With clear understanding of strengths of different sectors

National Programme for third sector commissioning (2006)

Commissioning is defined as the cycle of assessing the needs of people in an area, designing and then securing an appropriate service

Procurement comprises the aspects of the commissioning cycle focusing on the process of buying services, from advertising to contracting.

❶ Engage with third sector organisations to access specialist knowledge of user needs
❷ Consult potential providers well before commissioning, to set priority outcomes
❸ Put outcomes for users at the heart of the strategic planning process
❹ Map wide range of providers to understand their potential contribution to outcomes
❺ Consider investing in capacity of provider base
❻ Ensure contracting processes facilitate involvement of broad range of suppliers
❼ Seek to ensure long-term contracts and risk sharing wherever appropriate
❽ Seek feedback from stakeholders on effectiveness of commissioning process

Impact of contracting out of services

❑ Compulsory Competitive Tendering (CCT): tenders for provision of public services to be invited from private contractors, in competition with in-house provider.

❑ Formation of Direct Service Organisation, separate from client, to manage tender

❑ Extension of CCT to progressively wider range of local govt services 1979–1992

❑ Most contracts awarded in-house: impact = competition, rather than externalisation

Reported benefits of contracting out *(Chaundy & Uttley)*:

❑ Cost improvement (despite transaction costs) due to improved management, revised working practices, changed conditions of service, reduced labour
❑ Clarification of service requirements
❑ Greater focus on recipient of public services as customer
❑ Improved management and monitoring of service delivery
❑ Greater transparency about cost of central admin and support services

Arguments for contracting out	Arguments against contracting out
In-house focus on core competencies	Costs of market testing, tender process
Leverages external competencies	Lack of skills for contract management
Reduced costs (incl. direct purchases)	Potential neglect of service quality
Potential quality/performance gains	Impact on internal jobs, conditions, morale
Flexible capacity + innovation potential	Loss of control over key competencies
Faster service development	Efficiency gains uneven in practice

Impact of Best Value

Central government	• Develop 'modernised, high quality, efficient, responsive, customer-focused central government services' • 'Work in partnership with the private sector, extending the circle of those involved in public service' • Existing market testing policies to continue, *unless* better VFM can be achieved by other means (within running costs ceilings)
Local government	• Duty of best value: 'local authorities to meet the aspirations of local people for highest quality and efficient services possible within the resources available' (*Modernising Local Government*) • Recognition of costs/dysfunctions of CCT >> reduced detailed prescription; encouragement of partnership with private sector; 'fair employment agenda'

Impact of the Private Finance Initiative (PFI)

Public Private Partnership (PPP) is an umbrella term covering a variety of collaborative arrangements between public bodies and private companies in long-term partnership.

A **Private Finance Initiative (PFI)** is a form of PPP in which the private sector contractor finances the project, gaining return on investment via revenues from use of the asset over the contract period. On expiry, ownership may remain with the contractor or transfer to the public sector.

❑ Various Design, Build, Finance, Operate (DBFO) + ownership arrangements

❑ PFI should only be used where it can meet VFM, equity (eg in staff terms and conditions) and accountability commitments (*HM Treasury guidance*)

Advantages of PPP/PFI	Disadvantages of PPP/PFI
Secure funding for large-scale projects	Risk of lower public accountability
Co-opt private sector skills > VFM	Possibly lower levels of service
Incentivises high service levels	Impact on jobs, wages/benefits
Access expertise, resources, technology	Risk of 'lock in' with incompatible partner
Faster project completion > cost savings	Risk of reputational damage
Private partner may reap high returns	Does not always offer best VFM (NAO)

Procurement in central government

Organisation of Procurement (1993):

Key success factors	Progress
Clear strategy	Department strategies (*Setting New Standards*, 1995)
Info/control systems	Integrated procurement systems; Government Purchasing Card; e-procurement platforms
Development of expertise	Staff training; CIPS qualification; Government Procurement Service (GPS) > develop best practice
Input to corporate management	Contribution via efficiency improvements, contracting out, market price forecasts and expenditure profiles Appoint departmental Directors of Procurement
Entrepreneurial approach	Early involvement; use of service level agreements; procurement marketing; 'intelligent customer' development; cross-functional teams
Co-ordination	Central co-ordination via Procurement Group (PG)
Focused efforts	Leverage few, high-value transactions; rationalise supplier base and product ranges; devolved authority for low-value purchases

Procurement in local government

❑ No central co-ordination > power vested in functional departments/committees > purchasing role may be limited to procedural advice, clerical support

❑ Purchasing consortia > savings from amalgamation of contracts, skill development

❑ Use of competition: used patchily (Audit Commission 2002)

Procurement in the NHS

❑ Massive expenditure > political interest > attention to procurement development. Competition to win business from trusts > more commercial approach, attention to local needs, procurement management services for specialised requirements

❑ 2000: NHS Supplies replaced by the Purchasing & Supply Agency (PASA): centre of knowledge and excellence; advice on policy and strategic procurement

❑ Supply Management Confederations (SMCs) and Collaborative Procurement Hubs (CPHs) to bridge gap between national (Agency) and local (Trust) purchasing.

❑ National Association of Health Care Supplies Management > improve performance

Culture and goals of public/private sector procurement

Area of diff.	Private sector	Public sector
Objectives	To increase profit	To achieve defined service levels
Ownership and control	Buyers > directors > shareholders	Buyers ultimately > general public
Stakeholders	Defined group	Wide range of needs/interests
Activity/process	Organisational capabilities and resources used to produce goods/services	Add value supplying outsourced/ purchased products or services (not usually production)
Law and regulatory environment	Activities regulated by company law, employment law, product liability law etc	Additional provisions eg EU procurement directives (CCT etc)
Competition	Usually strong, multi-firm	Usually no competition
Value for money	Reduce cost for profit maximisation.	Maintain/improve service levels within value/cost parameters
Diversity of items	Specialised stock list for defined product portfolio	Wide diversity of resources required for diverse services
Publicity	Strict commercial confidentiality	Confidentiality limited because of public interest in disclosure
Resource issues	Investment constrained only by opportunities available	Investment constrained by imposed spending limits
Information exchange	Private sector buyers do not exchange information, because of confidentiality and competition	Public sector buyers often exchange notes, use shared e-purchasing platforms, consolidate purchases etc.
Procurement policies and procedures	Tend to be organisation-specific. Buyers can cut red tape when necessary	Tend to follow legislative directives. Buyers often constrained to follow procedure
Supplier relationships	Emphasis on long-term partnership development where possible, to support value chain.	CCT: priority to cost minimisation and efficiency, at the expense of partnership development.

However, key issues increasingly common to both private and public sectors >>

- Developing standards for development of procurement professionals
- Greater application of strategic sourcing principles
- Development of e-procurement systems
- Drive to improve customer service, cost efficiency to maximise value for money
- Drive for corporate social responsibility and sustainability (including compliance with relevant law and regulation – common to both sectors, as well as specific to each).

Private sector best practice: partnership

Partnership sourcing is a commitment by customers/suppliers, regardless of size, to a long-term relationship based on clear mutually agreed objectives to strive for world class capability and effectiveness. *(CBI, DTI)*

Advantages	Disadvantages
Greater stability of supply and prices	Risk of complacency re cost/quality
Sharing of risk and investment	Less flexibility to change suppliers at need
Better supplier motivation	Possible risk to confidentiality
Collaborative cost-saving, improvement	Lock in to relationship as needs change
Access to supplier technology/expertise	Restricted by EU public sector directives
Joint planning and info sharing > efficiency	Costs of relationship management
More influence with supplier	Possible loss of flexibility and control

Application to the public sector:

❑ **Partnership with Competition:** supplier selection combining competitive tender with pre- and post-tender negotiation; limited number of suppliers per item; medium-term contract period; fairly formal contractual relations *(Erridge & Nondi)*

❑ Increasing flexibility re tendering procedures, budgetary controls and contract duration within framework of EU directives and CCT.

Private sector best practice: supply chain management (SCM)

SCM is 'the management of relations and integrated business processes across the supply chain... The links in the supply chain plan and co-ordinate their processes and relationships by weighing the overall efficiency and competitive power of the supply chain.' *(Jespersen & Skjøtt-Larsen)*

Benefits of SCM	Limitations of SCM
Reducing non-value-adding activities	Not answer to all cost/quality problems!
Reducing cycle times	Risks of dependence, over-investment
Motivated/focused suppliers	Resources required to develop suppliers
Resource/capability sharing > innovation	Requires internal/supplier support
Reduced total costs	Difficult to measure effectiveness
Strategic focus on customer value	Problems in fairly distributing gains/risks

Application to the public sector:

Likely to be useful for departments/agencies where:

❑ Existing supply market is organised as chain or network
❑ There are significant logistics or distribution aspects to the contract
❑ The procurement is high profile or sensitive: need for control

Otherwise, cost/complexity >> sufficient to seek assurance from key suppliers that *they* are actively managing supply chains to reduce costs and improve quality.

Private sector best practice: lean supply

 Lean thinking focuses on reducing costs and maximising added value through: quality improvement; elimination of waste (activities which add cost but not value); employee involvement; and collaborative supply chain relationships.

Key values of lean thinking
Specify value creation from customer viewpoint
Identify all steps across value stream (process map)
Ensure flow of actions that create value
Remove non-value-added steps from operations
Only make what is customer pulled, just in time
Practise continuous improvement + waste removal
Use cross-functional teams and involve employees

Lean techniques eg
Just in time (JIT)
Total quality management
Zero defects
Continuous improvement
Time-based management

Application to the public sector

- ☑ Concentration on core business, with contracting out of services
- ☑ 'Cost-down' initiatives
- ☑ Use of buying agencies (eg OGC Business Solutions, NHS CPHs)
- ☑ Collaborative relationships to access innovation and expertise (eg Healthcare Trusts)
- ☒ Financial investment in suppliers
- ☒ Long-term partnership relationships (v CCT)
- ☒ Collaboration with suppliers in setting strategic objectives

For more detail, see Table 3.2 (Local Government Lean Supply Model) in your Course Book

Private sector best practice: cost reduction

- ❑ Working closely with suppliers
- ❑ Performance measurement based on procurement efficiency, customer satisfaction, whole life costs and benchmarking (not just price, cost reduction/avoidance)

Best practice in the public sector   *Setting New Standards (1995)*

Need for improved practice in line with best performing private sector companies re:

- ❑ Integrated procurement processes, covering whole cycle of acquisition and use
- ❑ Better management of risk (especially through incentivisation of contracts)
- ❑ Use of cross-functional teams in specifying requirements and supplier selection
- ❑ Information sharing and collaboration between departmental procurement units
- ❑ Development of relationships with suppliers (competition/collaboration as appropriate to nature of requirements and market)
- ❑ Development of professional procurement skills
- ❑ Systematic performance measurement (eg Procurement Excellence Model)

Obstacles to implementation	Overcoming obstacles
Culture: existing power structures, resistance to change	Leadership and continuity > sustained culture/change management
Lack of status: no procurement involvement at a strategic level	Post senior staff to high profile organisations; procurement marketing
Lack of expertise: eg in market/cost analysis, supplier relations, business view	Develop skills; provide career path incentives for qualified staff
Lack of resources: informational, human, systems	Improve management information; empower qualified staff; integrate systems
Risk aversion: propriety/regularity, regulations, audit and oversight	Proportional risk management; engage with auditors; apply regulations creatively; engage the market early

Improving skills and competencies

Core Competencies Framework	❑ Develop relationships with customers and other groups ❑ Apply and encourage others to apply best practice ❑ Negotiate with customers and suppliers ❑ Apply public procurement principles and legal requirements ❑ Prepare tender and contract documents ❑ Secure best performance from contractors ❑ Understand prices, estimate costs and identify/manage risk ❑ Understand markets
CPD	Certificate and Diploma of Competence (GPS & CIPS)
Successful Delivery Skills Framework	Electronic repository of OGC policy and Best Practice Guides on website and CD-ROM.
Successful Delivery Skills Programme	❑ Skills framework: skill requirements for effective project delivery ❑ Maturity matrix: benchmark skills for key roles on projects
Byatt Report (2001)	Local government need to: identify skills needed; set out strategy to meet needs (including recruitment, training, retention) Improvement and Development Agency (IDeA) and LG Employers' Organisation (EO) to lead in training programme development
IDeA Knowledge	Training and development initiatives: management and project procurement skills frameworks, best practice case studies, procurement training programmes

The public accountability system

- **Public Expenditure Survey (PES)**: aims to estimate departmental spending over three years: firm targets for Year 1; adjustable targets for Years 2 and 3.

- Departments submit **estimates** (based on previous year's expenditure + inflation + new policies) for consideration by Treasury and departmental officials, then by the interdepartmental PES committee.

- Final PES is **announced** at end November (with annual Budget announcement)

- Spending **authorised** by Parliament, via Commons' vote on Estimates

- End of financial year: departmental spending **audited** for propriety and VFM

- Ministers and officials may be questioned by the **Public Accounts Committee** on any reported areas of concern.

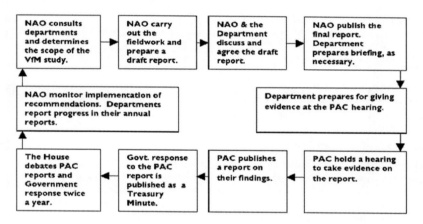

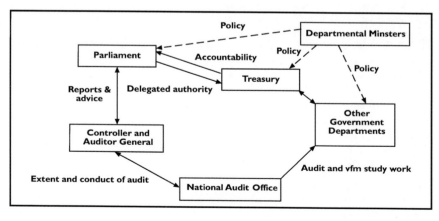

Role of the accounting officer

The **Accounting Officer** is normally Permanent Secretary of a department, Chief Executive of an agency/NHS trust or Chief Officer of a local authority. (S)he is responsible for ensuring regularity and propriety *[>> Unit 1.1]*.

Regularity (compliance)	Propriety (conduct and governance)
• Internal audit arrangements: Audit Committee, Statement of Internal Control (SIC) • Risk management framework • Audit trail (to track decisions) • Appointment of procurement director • Performance monitoring system (VFM, project progress, anti-fraud measures) • Monitoring progress v initiatives and external requirements • Reporting to PAC hearings	• Put in place and follow clear procedures • Get approvals where required • Don't allow conflict of interests to affect, or appear to affect, decisions • Don't use public money for private benefit • Record the reasons for decisions

Role of the Public Accounts Committee

❑ Considering the accounts and reports of the Comptroller & Auditor General (G&AG) laid before Parliament

❑ Auditing and scrutinising the probity of expenditure and VFM

❑ Sending for persons, papers and records to investigate areas of concern

Audit and Accountability for Central Government (2002)

❑ National Audit Office (NAO) to audit all non-Departmental public bodies (NDPBs)
❑ NAO to have legal powers of access to documents held by external bodies
❑ NAO to validate data systems used to report on Public Service Agreement targets
❑ Supporting arrangements to promote quality/transparency of central govt. audit.

Impact of accountability on procurement

❑ Delegated responsibility (eg for signing the SIC)
❑ Fear of critical reports by C&AG and National Audit Office (NAO)
❑ Threat of appearing before Public Accounts Committee

>> **Risk avoidance culture** >> 'over-protective' behaviour potentially reducing VFM eg:

☒ Rigid application of procedures
☒ Use of same terms and conditions, regardless of requirement, market conditions etc
☒ Reluctance to involve procurement at an early stage
☒ Reluctance to use innovative approaches (eg early dialogue with suppliers)
☒ Reluctance (eg by Finance) to expand the use/coverage of purchasing cards

Need to 'manage risk, not obviate it' (Treasury, 2000)   *[>> Unit 3.1]*

2.1 **Value and components of procurement spend** Course Book Chapter 4	**2.2** **Analysis of spend by market sector** Course Book Chapter 5

- Government
  departments and
  agencies
- Local government
- NHS

- *Value, frequency, volume*
- *Impact of spend on capacity
  and competitiveness*
- *Policy implications*

2.0
**Value and scope
of procurement**

Key roles

2.3 **Roles of key decision-makers in the procurement process** Course Book Chapter 6	**2.4** **Roles of key organisations in the procurement process** Course Book Chapter 7

- *Elected representatives*
- *Officials*
- *Impact of devolution*

- *Policy/co-ordinating organisations*
- *OGC*
- *NHS PASA*
- *IDeA*
- *Centralised/collaborative
  procurement*

Major components of public procurement spend

Public procurement is defined as the 'whole process of acquisition from third parties [covering] goods, services and construction projects. This process spans the whole lifecycle from initial concept and definition of business needs through to the end of the useful life of an asset or end of a services contract.' *(Gershon)*

Direct purchases: acquisition of goods and services	Capital projects: • Conventionally funded • Private Finance Initiative (PFI)	Disbursement of grants	Franchises Licences *(counted as income)*

Controllable procurement expenditure is more narrowly defined (Treasury Procurement Group) as all *non-pay running costs* and all *capital expenditures* influenced by the procurement function (rather than managed by budget holders or specialist groups). Grants and other non-contractual payments, and whole life costs, are excluded.

⮥ **Central government departments/agencies,** excluding NHS and Defence: £15 billion (NAO, 2004)
⮥ **NHS:** £17 billion (www.pasa.doh.gov.uk)
⮥ **English local government:** £31 billion (1999/2000, Audit Commission)

Sources of data on procurement spend

Data on procurement spend is important as:

* Second largest element of most organisations' spend (after pay)
* Useful element in public expenditure control: reflection of VFM, capacity to meet user requirements and fulfil policy priority.

NB:

❏ Different sources, definitions and methods of calculation in estimates

❏ Difficulties accounting for PFI projects. Supposed to have a neutral impact on public expenditure BUT value included in spend (based on construction costs, fees?)

❏ Absence of mechanisms 'to capture and analyse spend information in a way which enables Management Boards to understand what their departments are buying, and from whom' (Treasury, 1998)

⮥ **Central government:** £20 billion 'controllable procurement spend' (Treasury, 1997/1998). Under broader definition – including non-controlled and non-procurement spend (eg grants) and PFI contracts – estimate much higher: over £100 billion (Gershon, 2004), perhaps £150 billion per annum (Simms Report, 2006, based on analysis of National Accounts).

> The **Subjective Return Analysis (SRA)**, submitted to the Office of the Deputy Prime Minister, is an estimate of the breakdown of local authorities' pay costs and purchases of goods and services. It is based on actual data from a sample panel of some 120 authorities.

➲ English Local Authorities' non-pay spend estimated at £31.5 billion in 1999/2000: just over 50% of total spend (non-pay spend + employee costs).

Spend by product, service or project

Traditional emphasis on procurement of supplies > substantial increase in spend on services, following 1980s privatisation policy.

➲ 1997 average spend by departments and agencies:

34%	Goods (incl. IT equipment and consumables, stationery, furniture, clothing, vehicles, toiletries)
41%	Services (incl. IT, consultancy, transport, training, security, insurance, telecom, catering, cleaning, maintenance, travel)
13%	Capital
12%	Other (research, property rental, telecommunications)

➲ 2004 spend by central government departments and agencies (£15 billion):

19%	Accommodation
14%	IT
11%	Professional services (eg consultancy)
5%	Financial services
67%	Departments
24%	Agencies
9%	Non-departmental public bodies (NDPBs)

20% of departments, agencies and NDPBs account for 89% of expenditure.

➲ 1996/7 NHS Supplies expenditure (£2.5 billion) on behalf of trusts:

85%	Supplies (drugs and medical supplies)
10%	Services
5%	Capital

➲ 1998/9 English Local Authorities non-pay expenditure (£31.5 billion):

£8.1 b	Social Services
£6.8 b	Education

Value, frequency and volume of spend by market sector

- ☐ *Gershon, 2004*: 'underdeveloped understanding of the impact of new policies on the supply side, dynamics and characteristics of the supply markets'

- ☐ *Kelly, 2003*: steps to *increase competition* and *encourage long-term capacity planning* in markets where government has significant purchasing power

➲ 2001–2002 public sector spend as percentage of overall spend in UK

55.0%	IT
98.0%	Highways
31.1%	Construction (excluding some PFI projects)
12.8%	Professional services (public sector is second largest user)

Impact on capacity

Capacity relates to the volume of demand for a product, service or type of project that the total supply market can potentially provide.

Failure to provide long-range estimates of demand, to allow providers to plan supply

Lack of ability to plan for peaks/troughs in demand

Inability to identify aggregated demand

Factors likely to reduce market capacity

Reluctance to use Early Supplier Involvement

Lack of co-ordinated advertising between authorities

Lack of effective mechanisms for communicating with supply markets

Failure to publish contract award information

Inadequate information at time of advertising

Impact on competition and competitiveness

Competition relates to the number of suppliers in the market able and willing to supply requirements to the standard required.

Competitiveness relates to the ability of suppliers to win contracts, in competition with other suppliers, on the basis of price and non-price criteria.

Indicators of a market sector at risk of lack of competition	Factors lowering competitiveness
Share of supply purchased by public sector, and whether centralised	Large share of supply purchased by public sector
Level of/trend in concentration	High and increasing concentration
Extent of churn (supplier turnover)	Low levels of churn
Openness to imports	Low import penetration
Market growth, esp. private demand	Low growth in private sector demand
Entry barriers	High entry barriers
	Few substitute products/technologies
	Power imbalance between buyer/supplier
	Use of inappropriate procedures, reducing number of capable suppliers bidding

Office of Fair Trading, 2004

Sector	Potential concern re competitiveness
Sewage, sanitation, refuse disposal	Failure to exercise countervailing buyer power
Manufacture of weapons, ammunition	Restriction of competition in the short run
Human health activities	Failure to prevent (or contribution towards) reduction in competition
Building/repairing of ships and boats	Lessening of competition in the long term
Manufacture of pharmaceuticals, medicinal chemicals, botanicals	Failure to exercise countervailing buyer power to help overcome entry barriers and arrest increasing concentration
Manufacture of cement, lime, plaster	Failure to exercise countervailing buyer power

Audit Commission Report on Competitive Procurement (2002) in local government:

- ☒ Difficulty finding alternative delivery options because of weaknesses in supply market
- ☒ Choice of partners limited for smaller authorities
- ☒ Ineffective management of competition within the authority
- ☒ Lack of clarity about objectives, or resources available to meet them
- ☒ Non-existent or underdeveloped procurement strategies
- ☒ Inflexible standing orders and/or financial regulations
- ☒ Unrealistic expectations about immediate improvements

- ❑ Provide training for procurement staff
- ❑ Make effective use of specialist external advice
- ❑ Learn from project reviews

Policy implications

Kelly programme:

- ❑ Provide clear advance information on future needs
- ❑ Engage with key suppliers early (eg bid conferences)
- ❑ Take suppliers' needs into account in business planning (eg re changing needs, project delay/cancellation)
- ❑ Systematically pool market intelligence and info re projects/programmes >> better understand totality of public sector demand and capacity requirements
- ❑ Take more systematic/strategic approach to creating/managing major markets (eg shaping markets to protect competition and security of supply; adjusting demand or stimulating supply; involving OFT where competition is deemed inadequate)
- ❑ Ensure that procurement procedures, duration of contract and selection criteria are appropriate to the nature of the requirement and the market
- ❑ Departments to give a strong procurement lead to agencies and NDPBs in best practice (especially re market creation/management)

(eg)

CONSTRUCTION (2005)

- ❑ **Market consultation:** embedding early supplier engagement
- ❑ **Market shaping:** making and implementing market decisions based on specific regional pinch points and capacity issues
- ❑ **Market intelligence**: sharing supply/demand info for better future planning

---

WASTE MANAGEMENT

Stimulate competition (OFT, 2004) via:

- ❑ Contracts just long enough to enable suppliers to recover sunk costs (max 5 years)
- ❑ Open procurement processes
- ❑ Avoidance of overly restrictive selection criteria
- ❑ Supporting supplier access to necessary facilities (eg arrange access, acquire sites)
- ❑ Avoiding unnecessary aggregation of services (restricting number/type of bidders)
- ❑ Ensuring fair competition between in-house and private sector bidders
- ❑ Being aware of risks of collusion (eg monitoring results)

Develop capacity (OGC, 2006) via:

- ❑ Developing and publishing a 'co-ordinated picture' of authority plans and progress
- ❑ Developing a pool of procurement/project expertise/advice for authorities
- ❑ Publishing procurement timetables + benchmarking delivered outcomes

Democratic oversight of public procurement

UK: representative democracy – based on the role of elected representatives (MPs and local councillors).

Important to ensure **democratic oversight** of public procurement because of:

- Importance of public services in political decision-making
- Large amounts of public expenditure
- Increasing involvement of politicians/officials in supply markets

New Public Management reforms: limited role for politicians in allocation of contracts? Government's optimal role = 'intelligent customer' on behalf of citizens, purchasing privately supplied services so as to maximise the public welfare *(Dunleavy)*

Four strategic options for public sector reforms *(Pollitt & Bouckaert)*:

❑ **Maintenance** of existing relationships between political system, public administration and market economy (eg tightening traditional controls re expenditure, staffing, efficiency, fraud)

❑ **Modernisation:** more flexible methods in administration system > knock-on effects in political system

❑ **Marketisation:** introducing market-type mechanisms within the existing system of administration (eg through competition)

❑ **Minimisation:** transferring administration tasks to the market sector (eg through privatisation and contracting out)

>> Reform programmes (combining these elements) which ensure that key stakeholders exercise power in decisions >> win-win (or acceptable minimum) outcomes for all.

Mechanisms for political scrutiny of projects – collectively by ministers and MPs in Parliament – or individually by council committees > maintain democratic oversight. Eg:

- Scrutiny by MPS on Select Committees and the PAC of individual projects and overall departmental programmes
- MPs and local councillors: formal role in oversight over NHS, central department and agency projects within their area
- Provision for local referenda on programmes to provide a focus for political, community and stakeholder involvement.

Governance of public procurement

Seven Principles of Public Life *(Nolan, 1995)* as applied to procurement:

Principle	Definition	Procurement contexts
Selflessness	Decisions taken solely in public (not personal) interest	Avoidance/disclosure of conflicts of interest
Integrity	Avoidance of obligations that might influence decisions	Avoidance/disclosure of inducements
Objectivity	Choices made on merit	Transparency and competition
Accountability	Submission to public scrutiny	Accountability to Parliament for expenditure of public money
Openness	Transparent decisions/actions	Record (audit trail) of contract award decisions
Honesty	Declaring private interests	Avoidance/disclosure of conflict interests
Leadership	Promote principles by example	Uphold principles and CIPS ethical code

Responsibility/accountability for governance of procurement:

Central Government: policy & co-ordination	❑ Chief Executive of Office of Government Commerce (official level) ❑ Chief Secretary of the Treasury > Chancellor of the Exchequer (ministerial level)
Departments & agencies	❑ Procurement or Commercial Directors (larger departments) ❑ Chief Executive of NHS PASA > NHS Chief Executive > Secretary of State for Health (NHS) ❑ Permanent Secretaries, as Accounting Officers > Public Accounts Committee (in respect of reports by PAC) ❑ Permanent Secretaries, as Accounting Officers > Select Committees (in respect of specific sectors) ❑ Ministers may be asked to provide evidence to PAC and Select Committees, answer parliamentary questions or make a statement to parliament. ❑ Ministers with designated responsibility for procurement in Treasury and MoD.
Local government	❑ Minister for Local Government: overall responsibility for procurement policies eg Best Value ❑ Individual local authorities: allocation of responsibility may vary among members and officers ❑ National Procurement Strategy for Local Government (2003) advocated roles of member and officer procurement champions: member and officer with lead responsibility for procurement for their local authority.

Member Procurement Champion	Officer Procurement Champion
Instigating Best Value Reviews	Advocating strategic procurement
Championing corporate procurement strategy and alignment with Best Value Performance plan and community plan	Developing understanding of strategic procurement management with senior managers and officials
Promoting procurement vision	Advocating corporate procurement strategy and monitoring implementation
Promoting member skill development	
Championing procurement change	Championing procurement change
Oversight of executive responsibilities of officer champion	Advocating equality, sustainability, best practice, business case
	Overseeing performance of partnerships and key contracts
	Procurement performance management
	Procurement skills development planning
	Ensuring systems in place to oversee procurement and contract management
	Influencing choices re improving services

Impact of devolution

Devolution (transferred powers) > Scottish Parliament, and Assemblies in Wales and Northern Ireland >> different procurement approaches/practices.

Scotland:	Co-ordinated approach, reinforced by McClelland Report (2006)
N Ireland:	Central Procurement Division: expertise and contracting service
Wales:	Welsh Office – but local authorities and bodies have larger spend.

Issues eg:

❑ Opportunities for local bodies to **favour own policy preferences** (eg local or 'green' suppliers) enhanced by Best Value, and discretion in implementation of Directives (eg competitive dialogue, sustainability criteria).

❑ Increased **difficulty of maintaining uniform approach/standards** re:
- Compliance (eg via different Audit Offices, regional PACs)
- Collaboration (eg pressures to join regional rather than sectoral contracts)
- Use of non-commercial criteria for qualification and selection
- Increased pressure from local politicians/interests (eg to support local economy)

❑ **Scope for divergence reduced** by:
- Continuing co-ordination of audit policy/practice between regional audit bodies and NAO/Audit Commission
- Requirements of EU Procurement Directives and WTO's Government Procurement Agreement
- UK Treasury oversight of practice that reduces VFM, propriety or regularity.

Policy and co-ordinating organisations

Gershon Review (1999):

- Action required to achieve efficiency/modernisation/competitiveness objectives
- Problems in major government projects, especially construction and IT
- Inconsistent practices across government
- Recognition of growing dependence on purchased goods and services

- ❏ **OGC** to replace/extend role of Procurement Group:
    - Bring greater focus to the role of procurement in government
    - Consolidate existing central expertise in a single organisation
    - Increase accountability for deployment of central procurement resources

- ❏ **Supervisory Board:** top-level support and strategic direction: chaired by Chief Secretary to Treasury + senior officials from govt departs, outside experts and NAO.

- ❏ Reform civil procurement in central government, through:
    - Best practice techniques for VFM
    - Sharing knowledge between OGC and departments
    - Improving management of large, complex, novel projects
    - Facilitating commercial relationships
    - Developing strategic management of key suppliers and supply markets
    - Developing commercial skills
    - Developing optimum use of e-procurement

- ❏ Impact on machinery of government:
    - Direct, formal linking of central co-ordination of public procurement to public expenditure management/control (through role of Chief Secretary as Chair)
    - Linkage to wider government and policy (eg through Best Value and PPP/PFI)
    - Implementation of central policy in departments (via Supervisory Board)
    - Government Purchasing Service (within OGC) providing focus for professional and career development in procurement
    - Role of OGC in co-ordinating efficiency savings across the whole programme

The Office of Government Commerce (OGC)

- ❏ Priorities:
    - Improve public services by working with departments to help them meet their efficiency targets
    - Deliver savings in central government civil procurement, through improvements in success rate of programmes/projects and other commercial initiatives
    - Improve the success rate of mission-critical programmes and projects.

❑ Supporting improvement of:

- Efficiency
- Programme/project management
- Procurement

> **OGCbuying.solutions** is an executive agency of GC, providing procurement services to help public sector organisations and their private sector agents and contractors achieve value for money from procurement.

❑ OGC Gateway™ Review process (introduced 2001): mandatory for large, complex and novel procurements

> The **OGC Gateway ™ Process** examines programmes and projects at key decision points, and authorises progress to the next stage if the review determines that this can be done successfully.

❑ Framework agreements negotiated by OGC provide rationalisation of suppliers and prices in many sectors.

❑ NAO (2004) reported impact in improving departments' procurement, resulting in VFM improvements (approx 3.6% of total procurement spend over three years).

The NHS Purchasing and Supply Agency (PASA)

❑ Acts as centre of expertise, knowledge and excellence in purchasing and supply matters for the health service

❑ Advises on policy, strategic direction of procurement, and impact on healthcare

❑ Contracts on a national basis for products and services which are strategically critical

❑ Acts in cases where aggregated purchasing power will yield economic savings

> ➲   PASA works with around 400 NHS trusts and health authorities, and manages 3,000 national purchasing contracts, influencing around half of the £7 billion spent in the NHS on purchasing goods and services in the health service.

Objectives:

❑ Ensuring that changing requirements are identified and drive national P & S activity

❑ Ensuring delivery of results and targets through performance monitoring across NHS

❑ Developing provision of comparative info on P & S performance

❑ Maintaining overview of supply markets and advising on supply market issues

❑ Providing strategic direction to NHS Logistic Authority, to support supply strategies

Improvement and Development Agency (IDeA)

Provides tools and services to local authorities:

- ❏ Procurement competency framework
- ❏ Procurement training and development for members and officers
- ❏ IDeA Marketplace: e-portal and e-procurement service for local authorities
- ❏ Best practice guidance
- ❏ Procurement toolkit: basics, know-how and services.

Local Government Procurement Forum

Formed in 2003 to take forward development of national strategy.

- ODPM
- Local Government Association
- Govt depts with interest in local govt procurement (including HMT, OGC)
- Local govt central bodies (including Audit Commission, IDeA, 4Ps, Employers' Organisations)
- Supplier community
- Professional bodies (including CIPS)
- Public sector trade unions

Regional co-ordinating bodies

- ❏ Scottish Procurement Directorate (SPD) + eProcurement Scotland
- ❏ Value Wales (Procurement)
- ❏ Central Procurement Division of the Department of Finance (N Ireland)

Centralised/collaborative procurement

Advantages	Challenges
Significant economies of scale from pooling demand to command better deals	Diverse stakeholder needs: too great a choice of deals risks losing economies of scale. (OGC tries to offer optimum number of deals per spend category.)
Efficiencies: avoids duplicate tendering and framework development	Risk of distorting market competition, giving power to large suppliers
Increased buying power may help get wider policy priorities (eg sustainability) onto supply market agenda.	Sustainability: larger requirements may make it difficult for SME suppliers to compete. (OGC encourages SMEs to form own supply consortia to bid for business.)

Eg:
- ☑ OGCbuying.solutions central contracts for postal services, transport fleets, electricity
- ☑ Northern Housing Consortium
- ☑ Midlands Strategic Health Authorities Collaborative Procurement Hub (CPH)

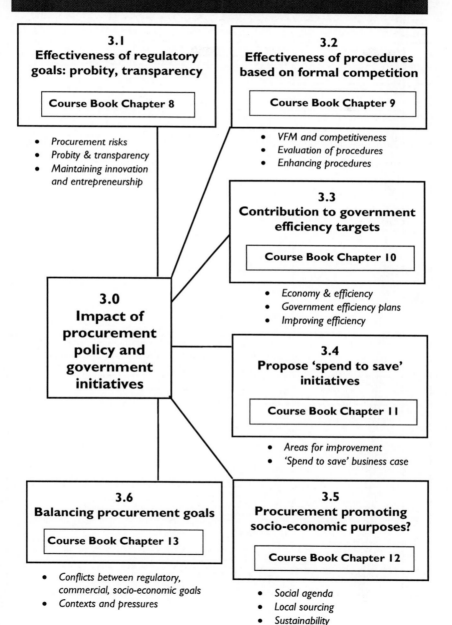

3.1
Effectiveness of regulatory goals: probity, transparency

Course Book Chapter 8

- Procurement risks
- Probity & transparency
- Maintaining innovation and entrepreneurship

3.2
Effectiveness of procedures based on formal competition

Course Book Chapter 9

- VFM and competitiveness
- Evaluation of procedures
- Enhancing procedures

3.3
Contribution to government efficiency targets

Course Book Chapter 10

- Economy & efficiency
- Government efficiency plans
- Improving efficiency

3.0
Impact of procurement policy and government initiatives

3.4
Propose 'spend to save' initiatives

Course Book Chapter 11

- Areas for improvement
- 'Spend to save' business case

3.6
Balancing procurement goals

Course Book Chapter 13

- Conflicts between regulatory, commercial, socio-economic goals
- Contexts and pressures

3.5
Procurement promoting socio-economic purposes?

Course Book Chapter 12

- Social agenda
- Local sourcing
- Sustainability
- Diversity

General risks from procurement *(Orange Book)*

	Category of risk	Illustrations/issues to consider
External risks	Political	Change of government, cross-cutting policy decision: machinery of government changes
	Economic	Ability to attract/retain staff; exchange rates affect costs; effect of global economy on UK economy
	Socio-cultural	Demographic changes affect demand for services; stakeholder expectations change
	Technological	Obsolescence of current systems; cost of procuring best technology; opportunity arising from development
	Legal/ regulatory	EU regulations which impose requirements (eg health and safety, employment legislation)
	Environmental	Building, disposal of waste/surplus etc need to comply with changing standards
Operational risks	*Delivery*	
	Service/product failure	Fail to deliver the service to the user within agreed/set terms
	Project delivery	Fail to deliver on time/budget/specification
	Capacity/capability	
	Resources	Financial (insufficient funding; poor management; fraud) HR (staff capacity/skills) Information (adequacy for decisions; privacy protection) Physical assets (loss, damage, theft)
	Relationships	Delivery partners (threats to commitment; role clarity) Customers/Service users (satisfaction with delivery) Accountability (particularly to Parliament)
	Operations	Overall capacity and capability to deliver
	Reputation	Confidence and trust of stakeholders
	Risk management	
	Governance	Regularity and propriety; compliance with relevant requirements; ethical considerations
	Scanning	Failure to identify threats and opportunities
	Resilience	Capacity of systems/accommodation/IT to stand adverse impacts and crisis; disaster recovery/contingency planning
	Security	Of physical assets and information
Change risks	PSA targets	New PSA targets challenge capacity to deliver
	Change programmes	Threaten current capacity to deliver + provide opportunity to enhance future capacity
	New projects	Making optimal investment decisions; prioritising between projects competing for resources
	New policies	Create expectations where the organisation has uncertainty about delivery

Factors in public sector risk management

Risk management is 'the process whereby organisations methodically address the risks attaching to their activities with the goal of achieving sustained benefit within each activity and across the portfolio of all activities' *(Institute of Risk Management)*

- ☐ Not motivated by profit motive: less likely to take investment risks for opportunity

- ☐ Low risk appetite (high risk aversion): accountability to taxpayer funders, scrutiny by public and media, external oversight (eg by NAO/Audit Commission), regulation

- ☐ No 'terminate' option despite high risk demands (eg hospitals, police, armed forces)

- ☐ High level of accountability: due process/diligence to ensure best value, service levels

- ☐ High compliance risk: detailed procedures, policy/regulation

- ☐ Wide range of activities > diversity, changeability, unpredictability of threats (eg armed forces in theatre of war)

- ☐ Public scrutiny: reputational risk, loss of confidence, political pressure, loss of funding

- ☐ Wider, more diverse range of key stakeholders in decisions

Using probity and transparency to manage risks

Public procurement regulations (transparency) and accountability systems (probity):

☑ Ensure that procurement activities meet requirements of propriety and regularity	☒ Reinforce formal procedures, restrictive interpretation of rules
☑ Minimise risks of discrimination and fraud *[>> Unit 1.1]*	☒ Cumbersome, time-consuming compliance with prescriptive rules
☑ Minimise political/reputational risks of *lack* of propriety/regularity	☒ Encourage a risk-avoidance culture
☑ Minimise compliance risks of breaching legal requirements	☒ May support lack of expertise and professionalism
☑ Reduce delivery risks through support for fair and open competition, VFM	☒ May result in unsustainable allocation of risk between client and contractor
	☒ Create obstacles to partnership relations with suppliers/contractors
	☒ Discourage innovation, entrepreneurialism, flexibility
	☒ Discourage leverage of procurement for wider socio-economic benefits

>> Risk management frameworks emphasising that: 'the purpose of control is to contain risk rather than to obviate it' (Treasury, 2000)

>> Meet intentions behind formal procedures, but support innovative approaches to design of contracts, supplier selection etc taking into account the nature of requirement and supply market.

'Managing rather than obviating risk' (Treasury, 2000)

'The NAO, PAC and Government have stated that they support **well thought through and well managed risk taking**. This increased emphasis on good risk management highlights the importance of ensuring that departmental **internal control systems** are based on a proper **risk assessment**. That, in turn, places additional emphasis on the Accounting Officer's responsibility to put in place **governance arrangements** that will ensure that this process takes place.' (OGC)

Management of Risks (OGC):

❑ How risks are identified
❑ How information about probability and impacts/consequences is obtained
❑ How risks are quantified
❑ How options to deal with risks are identified
❑ How decisions on risk management are made and implemented
❑ How actions (and the process as a whole) are reviewed and evaluated
❑ How stakeholder communication and engagement are managed

The Orange Book (HM Treasury)

❑ Identifying risks
❑ Assessing risks
❑ Risk appetite
❑ Addressing risks
❑ Reviewing and reporting risks
❑ Communicating and learning

Not just within the focal organisation but within the 'extended enterprise': the interdependent network of suppliers, contractors and other stakeholders.

Local government (Byatt, 2001)

'Local authorities should review their standing orders to ensure they **promote efficient and effective procurement** whilst **maintaining safeguards** of probity and good governance. Standing orders should be used positively to encourage good practice. Changes to standing orders should be accompanied by an effective education programme.

The Audit Commission should guide and train auditors and inspectors to **support a strategic approach to procurement** [emphasising] **a risk-based approach.**'

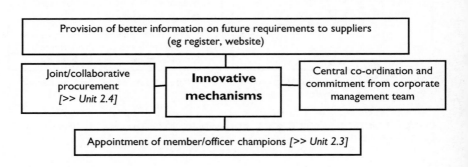

Competition and competitiveness

Competition relates to (a) the number of current (or potential) suppliers in the market able and willing to supply requirements to the standard required and (b) commercial rivalry between suppliers to win contracts. This is said to be the best guarantee of quality and value for money.

Extent of competition in a market (*Porter*) arises from **five forces:**

- Power of existing suppliers • Power of existing buyers • Threat of new entrants
- Threat of substitute products/processes • Intensity of rivalry

'Without market discipline [competitive mechanisms], civil servants have no incentive to control costs and are likely to expand production beyond socially optimum levels to maximise their own rewards in terms of status, power and income' (*Erridge & McIroy*).

>> Competitive tendering
>> Market testing
>> Contracting out
>> PFI/PPP

Formal competition-based mechanisms designed to secure cost reduction/savings and operating efficiencies

Competitiveness relates to the ability and willingness of suppliers to supply requirements in such a way, and on such terms, as to be successful against commercial rivals or market benchmarks.

Competitive supply therefore refers to the extent to which any supply arrangement provides supply which matches or exceeds requirements, at a cost which represents best value in relation to relevant competitive markets.

Competitive supply results from (eg):

- ☐ Buying in a contestable market: credible competition between two or more suppliers
- ☐ Leveraging availability of substitute products/processes
- ☐ Leveraging low switching costs (avoiding transaction-specific investments)
- ☐ Doing business with world class suppliers
- ☐ Collaborative buying to leverage higher volumes
- ☐ Organisational learning and improvement
- ☐ International sourcing: low wage, favourable exchange rates > lowest cost supply
- ☐ Minimising obstacles to competition, new entrants
- ☐ Trust between buyer and potential suppliers
- ☐ Supplier collaboration and commitment to continuous improvement

---

Value for money (VfM)

VfM is 'not about achieving the lowest initial price: it is defined as the optimum **combination of whole life cost and quality** to meet the customer's requirements' (*OGC*).

Whole life costs	Research	Planning	Design/spec
	Construction	Acquisition	Cost of finance
	Commissioning	Operating	Depreciation
	Maintenance/service	Decommissioning	Disposal

*Pre-acquisition * Acquisition * Operating * Maintenance * End of life*

Option evaluation when procuring assets: investment appraisal, make/buy decisions
Decision making to minimise whole-life costs: asset management planning
Balancing whole-life costs against specified quality: optimise specification.

Compare **traditional measures** based on **prices paid, savings data**:

- ☑ Partial measure of economy/efficiency contributions of procurement
- ☑ Politically advantageous: meeting public expenditure targets etc

- ☒ Little consideration of: complex procurement situation (*Ringwald*); 'added value' (*Dumond*); 'modern' procurement activities eg SCM (*Butler*).

Does formal competition achieve VFM and competitiveness?

Yes if:	Not necessarily, if:
Widens potential supplier base	Results in restrictive procedures
Stimulates competitive price, quality or innovation	Inhibits innovation and flexibility
	Inhibits co-operative supply chain practices
Discourages existing supply complacency	Procedures restrict supplier access
Protects v fraud, exploitation of power	Increases transaction costs
Minimises compliance risks/costs	Takes place in non-competitive markets
	Poorly managed

eg:

- ☒ Difficulties gaining access to info necessary to prepare bids
- ☒ Problems identifying/interpreting tender notices
- ☒ Excessive tender documentation and high bid costs
- ☒ Inappropriate standards and technical specifications
- ☒ Unclear delivery requirements or vague selection criteria
- ☒ Poor feedback from contracting authorities
- ☒ Buyer suspicion (risk aversion, lack of commercial expertise)

Evidence suggests formal competition requirements relatively unsuccessful in:

- ☒ Achieving greater cross-national competition
- ☒ Achieving VfM and efficiency (price competition offsetting increased transaction costs)

>> **EU Consolidated Directive** modernises requirements by introducing:

- ❑ Competitive dialogue process (>> early supplier involvement, collaboration)
- ❑ Provision for e-purchasing and electronic auctions (>> reduced transaction costs)
- ❑ Flexibility in applying frameworks and standard form contracts
- ❑ Debriefing process (>> improvements in future contracts)

'Buying goods and services through competition remains the best way of ensuring the best price for the quality of service required. But it is not always appropriate nor cost-effective for low-value items; complex goods and services; or where no well developed market exists.' *(Modernising Procurement, NAO, 1999)*

>> Combining competition with innovative ways of procurement
>> Managing risks associated with innovation
>> Drawing on latest advances in e-commerce and good procurement practice.

Innovative mechanisms to adapt formal procedures

Elements of private sector best practice   *(Erridge & Greer)*

❑ Early involvement with customer and suppliers
❑ Co-operative rather than adversarial supplier relationships
❑ Greater emphasis on contract management
❑ Use of cross-functional teams
❑ Strategic creation, development and management of supply markets
❑ Whole life costing in value definition and accounting

Procurement strategy   *(NAO, 1999)*

❑ Analysis of key goods/services, and costs, required to deliver outputs
❑ Assessment of how goods/services are purchased
❑ Performance of key suppliers
❑ Scope for price reductions and improvement in quality of service
❑ Scope to adopt innovative approaches while reliably managing associated risks

Early procurement involvement

'Ensure that procurement professionals are brought in at the earliest stages of projects, where their skills and knowledge are likely to have most impact' (Treasury, 2007) eg on contract specifications and performance review criteria.

☑ Supply market awareness (potential suppliers, technologies, risk factors etc)
☑ Evaluation of requirements in relation to supply factors
☑ Contacts > early supplier involvement
☑ Commercial/legal expertise for contract/specification development
☑ Purchasing disciplines > variety/cost reduction, value analysis etc

Early supplier involvement

• Communicate clear procurement objectives to potential suppliers at an early stage
• Gauge market's ability to deliver
• Explore a range of possible solutions: gain supplier input to specification, alternative materials or methods etc
• Consider output/outcome based specification, to allow scope for innovative solutions
• Communicate procurement process to potential suppliers at the outset.

Advantages of ESI	Disadvantages/problems of ESI
Quicker development lead time	Longer lead time, if conflicted/inefficient
Improved product specifications	Costs of communication
Better quality, lower development costs	Compromise transparency/competition
Access to new technologies	'Lock in' with incompatible supplier
Shared expertise for problem-solving	Potential for conflict: different agendas
Building trust, alliance, supplier loyalty	Risk if supplier/technology is unfamiliar
Better understanding of supplier capabilities > future partnership	Risk if products or services are designed around the supplier (dependency)

Use of e-procurement

E-tendering is the carrying out of competitive tendering process using electronic means.

E-auction is 'the use of an electronic device for presentation of new *prices*, revised downwards, and/nor new *values* concerning [non-price] elements of tenders, which occurs *after* an initial full evaluation of tenders, enabling them to be ranked using automatic evaluation methods' (EU Directive)

☑ Facilitates management, co-ordination, streamlining of tendering process
☑ Significant potential cost savings from price improvement and efficiencies
☑ Supports aggregation of demand (collaborative procurement)
☑ Increases fairness and transparency of tendering process: standardised/synchronised communication; transparent, instantaneous negotiation
☑ Supports control: internal auditors able to review full contract history

Other e-procurement tools:

- **E-procurement platforms** eg Zanzibar e-marketplace (OGCbuying.solutions)
- **Procurement cards**

Improved management information

❑ **Strategic market creation, development and management**   *[>> Unit 2.2]*

Need for management information re external environment, conditions and competition in supply market, market pricing, total public sector demand, impact on market sectors and related policy objectives

❑ **Active contract management of high-value and strategic contracts**

Need for management information to monitor the performance of the contractor, and taking action quickly when delivery, price and quality are at risk (NAO, 1999)

❑ **Improved procurement efficiency**

Need for management information re requirements/specifications, suppliers, catalogues, price/specification comparisons, supplier pre-qualification data

Concepts related to efficiency

Economy involves reducing the cost of inputs (eg paying less for products/services) regardless of the effect on outputs.

❑ Lower prices for the resources needed to provide public services. (Suitable where cost avoidance or price leverage achievable, but may compromise output/quality.)

Cost or productive efficiency involves optimising the ratio of outputs (public services, schools, hospitals etc) to inputs (eg labour, equipment, buildings, supplies etc).

❑ Reduced quantity or different mix of inputs, whilst maintaining the same level of service provision (eg reducing staff numbers)

❑ Additional outputs, such as enhanced quality or quantity of service, for the same level of inputs (eg added value through collaborative cost/quality programmes)

❑ Additional outputs for an increase in inputs that is less than the value of the increased outputs (ie improved ratio of output per unit cost of input)

Allocative efficiency involves changing the balance of different outputs in order to increase overall output/income.

❑ Eg focusing resources on selected groups in order to reduce social problems/costs

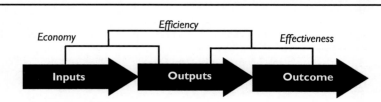

Lower prices for inputs
Reduced quantity inputs for same outputs
Additional outputs for same inputs
Additional outputs for small increase in inputs
Change in output balance for overall gain

Effectiveness involves achieving objectives or desired outcomes.

Issues in efficiency targets: cashable and non-cashable gains

Cashable gains are reductions in inputs (releasing resources for other use) which do not adversely affect the quality of outputs.

Non-cashable gains consist of increases in the quality of outputs, while inputs remain the same (not releasing resources, though using them more efficiently).

Cashable gains	Non-cashable gains
Inputs reduced; outputs maintained	Outputs increased; inputs maintained
Eg negotiated price reductions, collaborative buying, cost reductions	Eg negotiated quality improvements, added value
Risk: released resources may not be used efficiently	*Risk:* lack of resources to maintain increased levels of service
Benefit: 'hard' savings, released resources	*Benefit:* increased resource efficiency

'Some people say we should be looking at only the **hard cash savings**. Others say it is about getting **maximum value** for what we are spending. The risk of going to a pure cash savings regime is that you pull procurement into looking at price only and that is not where we want to be.' (Arminas, 2004)

Issues in efficiency targets: capital costs

'The majority of efficiency projects… require additional investment, including **capital costs** (such as new IT systems) that will enable the delivery of greater efficiency… Without matching of capital costs against gains, the target overestimates the efficiency gains that will actually be achieved.' (NAO, 2006)

Procurement contribution to efficiency strategy

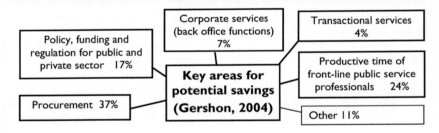

Policy, funding and regulation for public and private sector 17%

Corporate services (back office functions) 7%

Transactional services 4%

Procurement 37%

Key areas for potential savings (Gershon, 2004)

Productive time of front-line public service professionals 24%

Other 11%

Risks/issues for procurement	Opportunities for procurement
Centralised purchasing may disadvantage SME and VCO suppliers	Increased role in policy development through earlier involvement
Uneven implementation of proposals	Opportunities/funding for CPD, careers
Lack of procurement skill or qualification	Devolution of routine purchasing > focus on strategic market and supplier management
Procurement undertaken without professional support	
Lack of visibility/influence re total spend, strategic management of supply markets	Adoption of 'change agent' role: via PSAs, public expenditure/audit process
Long, onerous procurement processes inhibiting delivery	Greater role in delivering PFI/PPP projects and 'joined up' government
Cost-cutting role v best practice	Enhanced political role/status

Achieving and improving efficiency   *(Gershon, 2004)*

❑ Improve strategic market management (demand information, supplier engagement)

❑ Ensure that all procurement is conducted via processes put in place by procurement professionals *or* with direct support of procurement professionals

❑ Encourage shared procurement models (eg framework contracts, regional consortia), using incentive structure to encourage participation by devolved delivery bodies

❑ Enhance procurement capacity: leadership, professional expertise, best-practice tools (including e-procurement systems)

❑ Engage policy-lead departments to act as change agents/savings facilitators

❑ Improve VFM of direct and indirect procurement activity across delivery chains

Market	Planned contribution to efficiency savings via:
Construction	Market consultation, market shaping, market intelligence
Social housing	New partnering arrangements
Commodity goods	Aggregate demand across departments; framework contracts; e-auctions (eg energy, car fleet, temp staff, IT hardware)
Social care	Improved commissioning
Environmental services	Improved waste management improvement procurement (eg through ICT system improvements for commercial contracting)
Highways	Application of Highways Agency expertise
Defence	Modernisation of business processes
Education	Procurement Centre of Excellence to strengthen practice
Health	Leverage NHS buying power at the national level to gain VFM

Evidence of achieving improved efficiency   *(NAO, 2006)*

❑ 'Risk that efficiencies may not be measured accurately'

  ▪ Difficulties collecting spend data, quantifying process savings
  ▪ Inconsistency re treatment of capital costs and ongoing expenditure

❑ Major challenge of extensive, cross-sector change programme

❑ Risk that efficiency gains cause unintended falls in quality of service delivery

❑ Delivery dependent on key departments and procurement work stream

❑ Need for:

  ▪ Improved measurement of efficiency gains: baselines, inputs, outputs, audit trail
  ▪ Benchmarking of common practices
  ▪ Better data on efficiency and productivity
  ▪ Skills and capabilities to secure ongoing efficiencies

❑ Overall, considerable progress made towards efficiency targets, eg:

  ▪ Innovative 'contract for availability' awarded for Merlin helicopters
  ▪ Renegotiated national procurement contracts for NHS supplies/services
  ▪ E-auctions facilitated by Regional Centres of Excellence

Role of procurement in quality, performance and innovation

Contribution to quality

- ❏ Early procurement and supplier involvement > enhance specifications development, propose innovative solutions
- ❏ Clear quality specifications as basis for competitive tender
- ❏ Contract management (including requirement for suppliers to manage their supply chains for continuous quality improvement)
- ❏ Supplier/contractor relations > collaborative quality management, continuous improvement (based on 'partnership within competition')
- ❏ Data collection mechanisms allowing quality measurement/comparison/management
- ❏ Partnerships with expert private or third sector providers

Contribution to productivity/performance

- ❏ Sourcing strategies > reduction of purchase and transaction costs
- ❏ Contribution to make/do or buy decisions > effective contracting out of services
- ❏ Supplier relations > price leverage (competitive), joint cost reduction (collaborative)
- ❏ Development of e-procurement > streamlined processes, reduced transaction costs
- ❏ VFM based on whole-life costs + quality/service/socio-economic objectives
- ❏ Identifying opportunities for joint procurement

Contribution to innovation

- ❏ Capacity for innovation built into specifications, as basis for competitive tender
- ❏ Use of output/outcome-based specifications to allow innovative solutions
- ❏ Supply market info to highlight needs/opportunities (eg 'live' supplier database)
- ❏ Partnerships with private or third sector providers
- ❏ Longer-term contracts + equitable risk/gain sharing (> support investment in innovation)

>> Funding required for capital investment (eg in IT), staffing, skill development

Invest to Save Budget (ISB)

'Venture capital fund' for public sector service delivery, with an emphasis on innovation, efficiency and partnership working.

'Investment is provided in return for reform. The ISB is about promoting joined-up service delivery, forging new alliances, creating partnerships and promoting innovation by sharing the risks involved in new methods of delivery, so that users can receive the benefit of a more integrated package of services.' (*Treasury, 2006*)

Projects funded by ISB (eg:)

- Quality Measurement Framework Project (Office for National Statistics)
- 3D Procurement: Developing and Supporting Innovation in Public Sector Procurement from the Third Sector (Dorset Community Action)

Efficiency Challenge Fund

HM Treasury funding to help meet upfront costs of efficiency programme.

'The Challenge Fund money was made available for the Team's Change Agent activity to support departments in delivering efficiency gains. Funds have either been used to create central resources or have been allocated to specific projects at the team's discretion' *(NAO, 2006)*

Other 'Spend to Save' initiatives/projects

❑ Department of Health Independent Sector Treatment Centres (IS-TC) programme (2004): investment in efficient private sector capacity

❑ Plymouth Hospitals NHS Trust's Cardiothoracic Contract project (2002): contracting for cardiothoracic centre's entire needs > closer relations with reduced supply base, collaboration on needs identification, more efficient supply chain, stock availability, cost savings, patient focus.

Justifying 'spend to save'

Costs	Benefits
Upfront costs of financial investment	Improved communication/relationships
Costs of staff deployment/development	Improved technology/systems
Risks, challenges, time, cost of developing partnerships	Improved capacity/expertise
	Cost savings from joint procurement
Risk of project failure: poor functionality; suboptimal contract etc	Ongoing improvements from roll-out, reinvestment
Bureaucratic burden of proposals, management, scrutiny	Efficiency savings exceeding investment
	Improved service delivery
	Developing culture/skills for innovation

Proposal for a 'spend to save' project (including business case)

❑ Clearly identified lead organisation and Senior Responsible Officer (SRO)
❑ Details of other partner organisations
❑ Objectives of project aligned with relevant agendas, strategies, statutory agencies
❑ Clearly defined project objectives and expected outcomes
❑ Details of how project will benefit service users
❑ Evidence that the project is, innovative with estimate of amount of cash-releasing efficiencies deliverable
❑ Full economic appraisal (clear breakdown of costs)
❑ Details of project management arrangements and project key milestones
❑ Details of audit, monitoring and evaluation arrangements
❑ Robust risk management strategy
❑ Strategy for identifying and disseminating lessons learned
❑ Strategy for sustaining project once initial funding comes to an end

Using public procurement for socio-economic purposes

Arguments for	Arguments against
Market mechanisms alone may fail to deliver wider outcomes which are the responsibility of the public sector	Market mechanisms alone are sufficient to achieve socio-economic benefits:
Capacity building (eg by supporting SME/diverse suppliers, sustainability)	Distorts competition > uncompetitive supply and lack of VFM
Government mandated to pursue public interest *(Self)*	Risk of using contracts for political motives: abuse of democratic system
Increasing value of procurement: should be used for socially desirable goals	Potential for discrimination (illegal under EU regulations)
Diverse stakeholder needs to be met ('contested value')	Increased supply and transaction costs from use of non-commercial selection criteria
Moral responsibility to 'voiceless' stakeholders: social justice *(New)*	Lack of clarity/measurability re VFM in procurement contracts

Policy and legal context

❏ European Commission: objective of Single Market is to deliver long-term sustainable growth and job creation, with a strong economic rationale at its foundation.

❏ Original EU Procurement Directives allowed limited opportunities for social objectives:

- Contractors/suppliers can be excluded from tendering due to grave misconduct
- Contractual conditions can be adopted, where they do not modify original aim of contract *(ECJ: Beentjes)*

❏ At contract award stage, only two criteria allowable:

- Lowest price
- Most Economically Advantageous Tender (MEAT): limited scope to select between two or more economically equivalent bids on basis of condition or secondary criterion (related to combating unemployment: *ECJ: Nord-Pas-de-Calais*)

❏ Consolidated Directive (2006):

- Tenderers required to comply with law/regulation/agreements on social and employment protection
- Articles 48 and 49 (Economic and Financial Standing) modified to allow assessment of technical capacity of operators to deliver services/works that are (a) environmentally friendly (using EMAS certification) and (b) geared to health and safety of workers
- New criterion relating to environmental factors added to 'MEAT' evaluation *(ECJ: Concordia Bus v Helsinki)*
- Social factors which are (a) relevant to purpose of contract and (b) non-discriminatory may be taken into account in respect of disadvantaged groups.

❏ Local Government Act 2000: powers to promote economic, social and environmental wellbeing. Procurement to support local authority goals for sustainability, social cohesion and better quality public services (Byatt, 2001).

Social Issues in Purchasing (OGC, 2006)

☐ Sustainability requirements may be specified, where relevant to purpose of contract

☐ Requirements must be sufficiently precise > bidder understanding, contract award

☐ Eco-standards/labels can be specified, but equivalent alternatives must be considered

☐ Special conditions relating to performance may be specified, if (a) compatible with EC law, (b) mentioned in contract notice/specification and (c) relevant to contract.

☐ At selection stage, assessment of capability may include:

- Assessment of environmental management measures relevant to performance

- Certificates of compliance (eg EMAS) may be requested, but variants demonstrating equivalence must be considered

- Variant bids allowed where award based on MEAT criteria: minimum requirements must be specified

- Relevant contracts may be limited to 'supported' businesses/programmes employing mostly disabled people (stated in contract notice)

- Supplier may be excluded for proven non-compliance with env/social legislation

- Contract award criteria may include environmental characteristics, provided: (a) linked to subject matter of contract, (b) looked at from point of view of contracting authority (eg running/energy costs, environmental quality).

Meeting the requirements of different cultures

Race Relations Amendment Act 2002:

☐ 'Major obstacles to supplier diversity, [from] competition rules constraining the public sector's ability to positively discriminate in favour of specific groups of firms, based on characteristics such as location, firm size or the ethnicity of the business owner.'

☐ Imposes a duty on public sector agencies 'to ensure that their services are available to all communities... [and] to engage more actively with EMBs in a position to supply'.

Adapt the competitive tendering process *Commission for Racial Equality, 2003):*

☐ Consult local business, voluntary and statutory organisations on policy, procedure, advertisement of requirement

☐ Consider different packaging options to open bidding to smaller suppliers (NB rules prohibit deliberate splitting of contract to keep value below threshold)

☐ Advertise in a wider range of media, likely to be used by EMBs

☐ Make clear in notices/advertisements that consortium tendering is welcome

☐ Specify that all information relevant to contract/service is accessible to people with disabilities, ethnic minorities

☐ Specify that contractors responsible for new systems or services take all opportunities to make anti-discrimination recommendations

☐ Specify that any uniforms supplied be culturally sensitive

☐ Specify that contractor have procedures for dealing with complaints re discrimination

Supporting the sustainability agenda

Sustainable procurement is 'a process whereby organisations meet their needs for goods, services, works and utilities in a way that achieves value for money on a whole-life basis in terms of generating benefits not only to the organisation, but also to society and the economy, whilst minimising damage to the environment'. *(Sustainable Procurement National Action Plan)*

❑ Environmental/sustainable procurement policies, targets and action plans, supported by staff education and development

❑ Include sustainability criteria (eg energy efficiency, recycled content, biodegradability) at tender specification stage: not incompatible with VFM assessments (NAO, 2004)

❑ Consider ISO 14001 (eg NHS PASA) or equivalent standards/management systems

❑ Incorporate whole life costs/impacts in VFM assessment

❑ Engage and support **SME suppliers/contractors**:

- Utilise smaller contracts (below thresholds)
- Improve access to demand/contract info
- Engage via local business organisations and media
- Avoid over-specification (eg quality assurance certification)
- Encourage consortium bidding
- Encourage SME subcontracting by first-tier suppliers
- Prompt payment policy to protect financial viability

Public sector barriers *(Sustainable Procurement National Action Plan)*	
Identified barrier	**Recommendations**
Lack of leadership, clarity, ownership, poor incentives, mixed messages	Policy leadership, OGC support, clear and measurable targets
Priority proliferation, guidance overload	Rationalise policies and priorities
Failure to identify priorities, enforce minimum standards	Identify impacts, benchmark internationally, set mandatory standards in priority areas
Ignorance, confusion, lack of capability	MIS, training, Flexible Framework
Budgetary mechanisms do not enable/support sustainable procurement	Renew commitment to whole-life costing, quantify sustainability benefits
Lack of market engagement > innovation	Use Flexible Framework; improve risk/ relationship management; address SME/3rd sector capability; joint improvement

1. Benchmark performance: identify improvement areas (eg using Flexible Framework)
2. Identify priority areas of spend (based on risk assessment)
3. Rethink requirements: analyse business need
4. Engage stakeholders in design specification (eg early supplier/contractor involvement)
5. Aggregate demand (across organisation, through buyers, over time)
6. Use Quick Wins and Common Minimum Standards (guidelines for immediate gains)
7. Ensure management info systems are in place to measure sustainability benefits

Supporting the diversity agenda

- ❏ Legal compliance to combat discrimination or social exclusion
- ❏ 'Set asides': tender preference to diverse/minority-owned suppliers (US model of positive discrimination > potential favouritism, misuse, poor quality)
- ❏ Intermediary initiatives: brokerage to facilitate access of EMBs with large purchasers
- ❏ Building EMB capacity on a 'fit to supply' basis: overcome barriers to participation

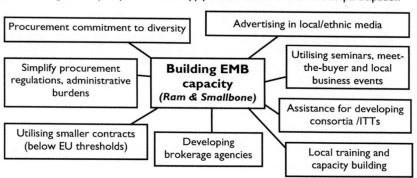

Local sourcing

Benefits of local sourcing	Drawbacks of local sourcing
Investment in community, employment, skills (plus reputational/brand benefits)	Materials, skills or capabilities may not be available locally (or may be more costly)
Supplier knowledge of local market, sustainability issues, regulatory standards	Smaller suppliers: no economies of scale (higher costs), greater dependency issues
Reduced transport, payment, cultural risks and costs	EU rules do not allow discrimination on basis of geography
Short supply chain: better delivery, fewer environmental impacts of transport	May not represent VFM

>> Need to develop strategies/policies taking both sides of argument into account – and carefully implemented/managed to minimise drawbacks/risks of chosen strategy.

Communities and employment

- ❏ Best Value review process requires community consultation and engagement: 'to empower communities to exert greater influence over the design and delivery of services' *(Geddis & Martin, 2000)*

- ❏ Employment Plans permitted as a contract condition/secondary evaluation criterion (eg Northern Ireland Unemployment Pilot Project):

  - ▪ Contractors required to include Employment Plan with bid, to be considered in event of 'tie' between two or more economically equivalent bids

  - ▪ Employment Plan: commitment to utilise unemployed in work on the contract

Multiple goals of public procurement

Regulatory goals	Commercial goals	Socio-economic goals
Compliance	Economy and efficiency	Social welfare
Propriety and regularity	Value for money/best value	Sustainability
Transparency	Innovation	Equity
Competition	Competitiveness	Diversity
	Procurement best practice	Public sector values/ethos

Potential goal conflicts

eg   Restrictive interpretation of regulations > failure to achieve competitive supply (eg by inhibiting innovation, partnership, wider supplier participation)

Possible resolution approaches

- ❑ Flexibility in applying regulations to encourage wide participation/innovation
- ❑ Partnership within competition
- ❑ Best value policy

eg   Restrictive interpretation of regulations > failure to support sustainability/diversity

Possible resolution approaches

- ❑ Adapt competitive tendering process, within regulations   *[>> Unit 3.5]*
- ❑ Build SME/EMB/sustainability capacity to compete   *[>> Unit 3.5]*

eg   Early involvement, partnership with suppliers to achieve competitive/innovative supply > reduce transparency, risk fraud, compromise compliance

Possible resolution approaches

- ❑ Compliance with regulations to protect transparency
- ❑ Internal controls to protect against fraud
- ❑ Partnership within competition

eg   Focus on socio-economic goals (eg 'set asides' for diversity, split requirements to provide contracts below thresholds) > risk breach of regulations

Possible resolution approaches

- ❑ Enforce compliance with regulations
- ❑ Clear guidance/education for all officers with buying responsibilities

eg   Focus on socio-economic goals (eg green procurement) > extra or hidden costs, compromising economy/VFM

Possible resolution approaches

- ❑ Emphasise mutual reinforcement (eg economic benefits of sustainability)
- ❑ Emphasise long-term VFM/cost savings (eg whole-life basis)

eg Focus on commercial goals (eg lowest price) > socio-economic/ethical costs (eg exploitation of low-wage workers, risk to supplier viability)

Possible resolution approaches

❑ Management of stakeholder perceptions, expectations and performance indicators
❑ Quantify costs of ethical/compliance risk
❑ Clear ethical sourcing/trading policies and supplier standards

Pressures to achieve conflicting procurement goals

❑ Culture of regulatory compliance

❑ Audit/scrutiny framework + penalties for non-compliance

❑ Public sector values/ethos re trust, equity, diversity, sustainability

❑ Needs/expectations of diverse stakeholder groups: taxpayers/voters, regulatory bodies, clients/customers, pressure/interest groups etc

❑ Political pressures + stakeholder influence (eg on funding, votes, media)

❑ Procurement professional standards (re ethics, sustainability, technical competence)

❑ Procurement performance measures (commercial/non-commercial measures)

❑ Desire for higher procurement status/influence (based on cashable gains?)

❑ Wider policy framework of national government (eg re sustainability, diversity)

❑ Wider policy framework of transnational governing bodies (eg EU, UN)

Evidence of achieving conflicting goals

eg **Unemployment Pilot Project (NI)** *(Erridge, 2007)*

Goals		Outcomes
Regulatory	Propriety	Compliant with internal and external risk management frameworks against fraud
	Transparency	Compliant with UK and EU procurement procedures
Commercial	Economy	Minimal additional costs to clients, contractors and taxpayers
	Efficiency	Input/output ratios demonstrate VFM
Socio-economic	Social welfare (equality, minority protection, sustainability)	Contractors better able to deliver social projects Unemployed gaining sustainable employment
	Public sector values (trust, legitimacy, equity, ethos, accountability)	Policy widely consulted on, developed jointly between clients, procurement and business; equality proofed Trust developed between contractors and clients

Transforming Government Procurement *(Treasury, 2007)*

Goals		Outcomes
Regulatory	Propriety	Compliant with internal and external risk management frameworks against fraud
	Transparency	Compliant with UK and EU procurement procedures
Commercial	Economy	• Better use of collective buying power • Better use of new procurement methods (eg Government Procurement card)
	Efficiency	• Increasing numbers of construction projects completed on time and on budget • OGC delivering efficiency savings • More intelligent procurement > shape the market > more innovative/effective products
Socio-economic	Social welfare	• Commitment to sustainable procurement (government estate carbon neutral by 2012) • OGC support eg expertise in valuing whole life costs/benefits
	Public sector values	• Taxpayers 'have the right to expect government to meet the highest professional standards when it procures on their behalf' • Innovative procurement methods and products/services > procurement built on principles of VFM and sustainability

eg   **Dorset County Council transport and eco-diesel policy**   *(IDeA, 2006)*

Goals		Outcomes
Regulatory	Propriety	Compliant fraud risk management procedures Compliant with EU emissions legislation
	Transparency	Compliant with EU procurement procedures
Commercial	Economy	• Reducing costs by aggregating vehicle requirements across the organisation • Environmental tax reduction benefits/grants
	Efficiency	• Selection based on whole life costs and various funding options • Reduction in waste through analysis of vehicle usage/tracking
Socio-economic	Social welfare	• More environmentally-friendly products/fuels • Recycling of vehicle parts • Local suppliers to reduce delivery costs
	Public sector values	• Health benefits of reduced toxic emissions • Reduced carbon footprint, resource consumption

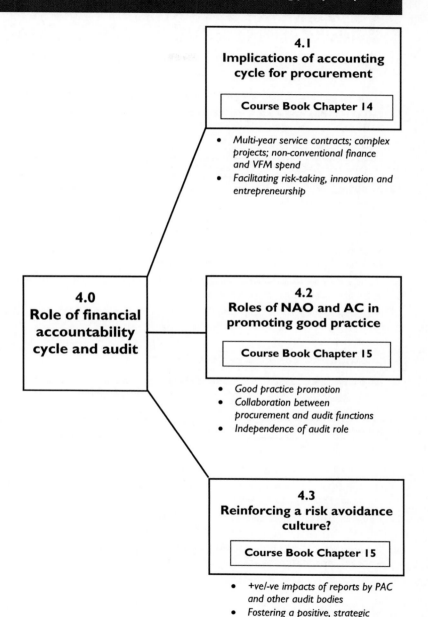

Learning Objective 4.0: significance of financial accountability cycle and role of audit for improving policy and practice

4.1
Implications of accounting cycle for procurement

Course Book Chapter 14

- Multi-year service contracts; complex projects; non-conventional finance and VFM spend
- Facilitating risk-taking, innovation and entrepreneurship

4.0
Role of financial accountability cycle and audit

4.2
Roles of NAO and AC in promoting good practice

Course Book Chapter 15

- Good practice promotion
- Collaboration between procurement and audit functions
- Independence of audit role

4.3
Reinforcing a risk avoidance culture?

Course Book Chapter 15

- +ve/-ve impacts of reports by PAC and other audit bodies
- Fostering a positive, strategic approach to managing risks

Government accounting cycle   *[>> Unit 1.4]*

- ❑ Set up to ensure accountability to Parliament for annual allocations of public funds
- ❑ Designed to achieve propriety and regularity, rather than VFM
- ❑ Designed on basis of controlling inputs rather than improving outputs/outcomes
- ❑ Growth in value, scope and complexity of public procurement > implications for parliamentary oversight.

Implications for multi-year service contracts

- ❑ Annual budget allocations: encouraged year-end spending by budget holders on unnecessary purchases
- ❑ Contract durations of ≤ 1 year (periodic re-tendering) used due to uncertainty over future allocations
- ❑ Strict cash limits on annual budget allocations > difficult to take advantage of additional volume or service quality improvements offered by suppliers
- ❑ Suppliers/buyers accustomed to annual increases in price (rather than cost/quality improvements over life of multi-year contracts)
- ❑ No incentive for suppliers to provide cost/quality improvements, due to risk of losing contract in next annual tendering exercise

Implications for complex projects

- ❑ Accounting system based on individual departmental allocations (rather than co-ordinated needs of complex projects with multiple participants)

Implications for non-conventional finance

- ❑ Difficult for Parliament to oversee PFI:
  - Capital cost not charged to public expenditure
  - Fees payable to contractors subject to commercial confidentiality (agreed prior to scrutiny of estimates/accounts)
- ❑ Complexity of calculation of bids by consortia, and fees payable to consortia, for long-term PFI contracts > beyond capability of accounting system to manage
- ❑ Government dependent on external financial consultancies to evaluate PFI projects with long-term implications for public expenditure

Implications for VFM procurement spend

❑ Business case for expenditure assessed by Treasury on basis of size of bid + departmental performance in staying within budget – not benefits/outcomes/VFM

❑ No mechanism for linking expenditure to departmental goals, desired outcomes

❑ Difficult to establish efficiency/effectiveness of procurement: broad category notes in accounts re expenditure – no provision for accurate link back to allocations

Encouraging risk, innovation and entrepreneurship?

Multi-year budgets

Framework for public expenditure now divided between:

❑ **Annually Managed Expenditure (AME)** eg social security benefits, local authority self-financed expenditure, debt interest, payments to EU institutions

❑ **Departmental Expenditure Limit (DEL)** spending

- Planned and controlled on a **three year basis**
- **Year-end flexibility**: carry forward unspent DEL provision to following year
- Designed to **cascade** from departments to executive agencies/budget holders
- DEL plans and annual limits (set in Spending Reviews) strictly enforced

☑ Certainty over medium-term budgetary allocation
☑ Stability to plan public service procurement on a 'sensible time scale'
☑ Minimise unnecessary year-end procurement
☑ Strong incentive to control costs and maximise VFM
☒ Annual limits may limit opportunistic purchases/improvements, inhibiting VFM
☒ Three years may be too short for longer-term service contracts

Expenditure planning

Comprehensive Spending Review (CSR):

❑ Assessment of what spend/reforms have achieved > new objectives

❑ Examination of key long-term trends/challenges > public service response

❑ Zero-based reviews of baseline expenditure > assess effectiveness v long-term objectives + release resources required to meet challenges + maximise VFM

❑ Embed/extend ongoing efficiency savings into departmental expenditure planning

☑ Longer-term perspective for procurement > stronger focus on goals/strategies
☑ Highlight and prioritise emerging goals/agendas eg sustainable procurement

Public Service Agreements (PSAs)

❑ Set out agreed targets for outputs/outcomes to be delivered by departments with resources allocated to them

❑ Government monitors progress v PSA targets: departments report in detail in annual departmental reports (spring) and performance reports (autumn)

☑ Increase transparency/scrutiny of goals, outputs, outcomes (at departmental level)

☑ Transparency of budgetary allocations > identify and 'ring fence' funds for procurement specific/supported measures > support development of procurement plans

☑ Targeted allocations > link to outputs/outcomes > measure efficiency/effectiveness

Capital expenditure

Departmental Investment Strategies (DISs):

❑ 'Coherent long-term strategy against which investment decisions are taken' (Treasury, 2004)

❑ Departmental plans to deliver scale/quality of capital stock needed to underpin objectives:

- Existing capital stock

- Future plans for stock

- Plans for new investment

- Systems in place to ensure effective delivery of capital programmes

Private Finance Initiatives (PFIs)

☑ Coherent long-term strategy for investment decisions

☑ Basis for long-term planning of projects, including PFI projects

☒ PFI projects: difficult to calculate service levels in advance > difficult to assess likely VFM of projects over 15–30 year period

Roles of the National Audit Office and Audit Commission

The National Audit Office	The Audit Commission
• Audits financial statements of central govt departments/agencies, and reports on VFM • Offers support and guidance: lessons learned from reports, case studies • Ensures weaknesses in public service delivery are continuously improved • Knowledge bank for risk management and PPM	• Assesses local public services in England (Comprehensive Area Assessment) • Central knowledge team and knowledge networks to strengthen good practice • Better Managed Information project to improve knowledge management • Offers case study info and guidance on performance/risk areas

Collaborative working between procurement and audit functions

'Auditors – both external and internal – have an important role to play in promoting improvements in procurement, particularly by adopting a constructive approach and highlighting good practice which can be more widely applied.'

(Getting value for money from procurement: how auditors can help: NAO/OGC, 2002)

Opportunity for forward looking and constructive approach by auditors to:

❑ Reviewing how departments and agencies *determine the need* for goods and services and how they *procure* them – to identify how this might be done better

❑ Highlighting *good procurement practice* which might be more widely applied

❑ Supporting *well-managed risk taking and innovation* likely to lead to sustainable improvements in cost of procurement and quality of purchases

❑ Ensuring that departments and agencies have overall organisational and management *capability* to undertake large, novel and/or contentious projects

Mechanisms for internal audit involvement/collaboration

❑ **Multi-annual audit**: review of overall procurement function

❑ **Assessment**: eg v Procurement Excellence Model

❑ **Annual programme**: issues/policies/systems agreed between procurement and audit for specific study

❑ **In-year studies**: unplanned/urgent/emerging issues (eg electronic procurement)

❑ **Pre-emptive advisory role**: ensuring appropriate/sufficient procurement competence involved at early stage in policy developments and major projects

❑ **Risk assessment**: checking procurement risk assessment and management carried out by project teams

❑ **Gateway review**: checking reviews carried out at appropriate stages of projects

❑ **Post-implementation review**: on-completion audit and/or at agreed stages of long-term contract, to check planned VFM benefits achieved, risks managed

Limits of collaborative working

Involvement/collaboration 'must be conducted with care so that:

☐ It does not prejudice the auditor's ability to conduct post-contract examinations [in terms of objectivity and independence of audit role]

☐ The audit regime does not slow up the procurement process.' (NAO/OGC, 2002)

☐ Potential audit emphasis on risk avoidance does not reinforce a risk-avoidance culture, inhibiting innovation, appropriately-managed risk taking, entrepreneurship

Promotion of good procurement practice

☐ **Leading practice:** Centres of Excellence, benchmark projects/organisations

☐ **Policy guidance:** guidance documents and template frameworks for PPM, sectors (eg construction, education) and policy themes (eg sustainability). Published by eg:

- OGC, National Audit Office and Audit Commission
- Regional Improvement & Efficiency Partnerships and Centres of Excellence
- Government departments

☐ **Exemplary material:** published case studies of successful project/programme delivery, risk management processes etc

☐ **Reports:** end-stage and post-completion reports on programmes and projects

☐ **Rules of thumb:** brief, informal guidance notes, process checklists and 'tips'.

Impact of audit reports on procurement

Modernising Procurement (1999)	Improving Procurement Value for Money (2004)

Improving Public Services through Better Construction (2005)	**Positive NAO reports highlighting best practice eg**	Progress in Improving Government Efficiency (2006)

However:

❑ Fear of critical reports by National Audit Office (NAO), Audit Commission (NHS) or local government auditors
❑ Threat of appearing before Public Accounts Committee
❑ Negative reports highlighting and publicising incidences of poor procurement practice

>> **Risk avoidance culture** >> 'over-protective' behaviour potentially reducing VFM, innovation, entrepreneurialism eg by:

☒ Rigid application of procedures
☒ Use of same terms and conditions, regardless of requirement, market conditions etc
☒ Reluctance to involve procurement at an early stage
☒ Reluctance to use innovative approaches (eg early dialogue with suppliers)

Need to 'manage risk, not obviate it' (Treasury, 2000)　　　　**[>> Unit 3.1]**

'Well-thought-through innovation and risk taking'

'The NAO will support examples of well-thought-through innovation and risk taking... NAO auditors would expect to find that:

• A full and reasonable assessment of risk has been carried out
• Proper procurement procedures have been followed
• Appropriate systems are in place for planning, monitoring and managing procurement projects.'

❑ Strategic approach to procurement and major procurements
❑ Senior level ownership of procurement issues
❑ Effective deployment of procurement expertise at an early stage of major projects
❑ Implementation of best practice
❑ Balancing regulatory, commercial and socio-economic goals
❑ Development of procurement skills (eg re market development and contract management)